John Owen

by Simonetta Carr

with Illustrations by Matt Abraxas

REFORMATION HERITAGE BOOKS

Grand Rapids, Michigan

John Owen
© 2010 by Simonetta Carr

Cover artwork by Matt Abraxas: Owen reading his Catechism to a family. For additional artwork by Matt, see pages 9, 15, 19, 25, 29, 31, 33, 35, 43, 45, 47, 51, and 53.

Published by
Reformation Heritage Books
2965 Leonard St., NE
Grand Rapids, MI 49525
616-977-0889 / Fax: 616-285-3246
e-mail: orders@heritagebooks.org
website: www.heritagebooks.org

Library of Congress Cataloging-in-Publication Data

Carr, Simonetta.
  John Owen / by Simonetta Carr ; with illustrations by Matt Abraxas.
    p. cm. — (Christian biographies for young readers)
  ISBN 978-1-60178-088-1
  1. Owen, John, 1616-1683—Juvenile literature. 2. Dissenters, Religious—England—Biography—Juvenile literature. 3. Theologians—England—Biography—Juvenile literature. I. Abraxas, Matt. II. Title.
  BX5207.O88C37 2010
  285'.9092—dc22
  [B]
                                        2010026554

For additional Reformed literature, both new and used, request a free book list from Reformation Heritage Books at the above address.

Printed in the United States of America
10 11 12 13 14 15/10 9 8 7 6 5 4 3 2 1

CHRISTIAN BIOGRAPHIES FOR YOUNG READERS

This series introduces children to important people in the Christian tradition. Parents and school teachers alike will welcome the excellent educational value it provides for students, while the quality of the publication and the artwork make each volume a keepsake for generations to come. Furthermore, the books in the series go beyond the simple story of someone's life by teaching young readers the historical and theological relevance of each character.

AVAILABLE VOLUMES OF THE SERIES
John Calvin
Augustine of Hippo
John Owen

SOME ANTICIPATED VOLUMES
Athanasius
Lady Jane Grey
John Knox
Jonathan Edwards
…and more

Table of Contents

A map of England during John Owen's time. As you read this book,
you may want to follow his travels on this map.

Introduction

John Owen (1616–1683)

John Owen was born in the town of Stadhampton, near Oxford, England, in 1616 and lived for sixty-seven years during a very difficult period of English history. Many people consider him to be the greatest English theologian (a theologian is someone who studies and teaches about God).

About a century before John Owen was born, when England was still a Roman Catholic country, King Henry VIII disagreed with the pope and set himself up as the head of the Church of England. All Christian communities in England had to be part of this church. To help people adjust to the change, some theologians compiled a book of prayers and rules, called the Book of Common Prayer. Many Christians thought that this book was good because it had excellent teachings, similar to those taught by Luther and Calvin.

Over the years, however, the Book of Common Prayer changed. By the time John Owen was born, some thought that its rules were too similar to those ordered by the pope and that the fancy clothes, ceremonies, and decorations the Church of England required or allowed distracted people from the main purpose of worship, which is the glory of God. Because they chose not to conform to (or accept) all these rules, they were called Nonconformists. Because they wanted to make their worship of God as pure and simple as it is in the New Testament, they were also called Puritans.

PHOTO BY MICHAEL CARTER, WIKIMEDIA COMMONS

Old Ship Church, Hingham, Massachusetts, built around 1635 by Puritans

PHOTO BY LORENZO FRATTI, WIKIMEDIA COMMONS

Roman Catholic cathedral in Milan, Italy

CHAPTER ONE

Growing and Studying in Difficult Times

PHOTO BY WILLIAM WELLS

St. John the Baptist Church in Stadhampton was built five hundred years before John Owen's birth.

John Owen's father was a Puritan pastor. He loved God and worked hard for Christ's church, teaching his children to do the same. Young John probably heard his father talk a lot about the importance of worshiping God just as the Bible teaches us to do. He also heard that many Puritans were leaving the country to go to lands where they could worship freely: some to Germany, some to Holland, and some to the New World, America.

John was very smart. When he was twelve, he entered college with one of his brothers, who was four years older than John. His studies were paid for by a rich uncle who encouraged him to make a good career in the Church of England. John studied hard, but he also found time for other activities, like playing the flute and performing the javelin toss and the long jump. All this kept him so busy that he had only four hours of sleep each night. Many years later, he said that he was sorry to have sacrificed his sleep because he had damaged his health.

In college, John Owen found time for many activities, like javelin toss.

While John was in college, many changes were troubling England. Some decisions made by the king, Charles I, caused his group of councilors (called Parliament) to become very angry. They didn't like that the king had demanded new taxes and had started a losing war against Scotland without talking to them first, as he had agreed to do. On the other hand, the king didn't always want to talk to the Parliament because he thought that they wanted to have too much power.

King Charles I (1600–1649)

The Puritans were also worried because the king had become very strict about the rules of worship, punishing hard those who refused to conform to the Book of Common Prayer. Someone who inspired and supported the king in his restriction of the Puritans was Archbishop William Laud, the highest religious authority in England, who disagreed with them even on the most important matters of salvation.

Archbishop William Laud (1573–1645)

PHOTO BY ERIC HARDY

An ancient building in Hurley, England.
John Owen lived in Hurley for some time
at the home of a local nobleman.

Soon after his graduation, Owen had to face a difficult decision. If he wanted to continue his well-respected career in the university and Church of England, he would have to accept many things he considered very wrong. Archbishop Laud had great influence at Oxford and was not only enforcing his rules of worship but also limiting what could be taught. Choosing to follow his convictions, Owen left the university and worked as a chaplain and tutor at the homes of some noblemen in the area. They were temporary jobs, which gave him time to think and study.

By 1642, the disagreements between King Charles and the Parliament had become so strong that the two declared war on each other. We call this the English Civil War, or English Revolution. A civil war is a war that is fought between people in the same country. Civil wars are usually worse than other types of war because the people are not united against an enemy, but are divided against each other. Owen thought that the Parliament was right, but the nobleman who had hired him at that time supported the king. Soon Owen decided to move to London, where he had relatives. At this point, even his uncle, a supporter of the king, stopped sending him money.

A battle scene of the English Civil War

Owen was discouraged. Not only was he poor and without a job, but he also had many questions about his faith. He wondered if God really loved him and if he was really one of God's children. One day he traveled with a friend to another town to hear a sermon by a famous minister.

For some reason, the preacher did not show up, and someone else took his place. Owen was disappointed. His friend wanted to leave, but Owen was too tired, so they stayed. The new preacher announced the title of the sermon: "Why are you fearful, O you of little faith?" Owen listened attentively as the Holy Spirit calmed all his fears through the preacher's words. He knew that through the life, death, and resurrection of Jesus, God had really adopted him as His son.

Owen listened attentively as the unknown preacher's words calmed all his fears.

CHAPTER TWO
A Pastor and a Writer

Finally sure of his salvation, Owen found new energy and courage. He spent the next months writing a book explaining why he believed that some of William Laud's teachings were not according to the Bible. As his book became famous, some people invited him to work temporarily as a pastor in the small country town of Fordham, in the beautiful Stour Valley. Owen loved his work and spent some of the happiest years of his life in that place. He was young and had the energy and passion to spend long hours teaching, preaching, and visiting his church members regularly. Two years later, he met and fell in love with a young woman named Mary Rooke, who soon became his wife. He later wrote that she was "excellent and comely [pretty]," and that they loved each other with affection.

The Stour Valley

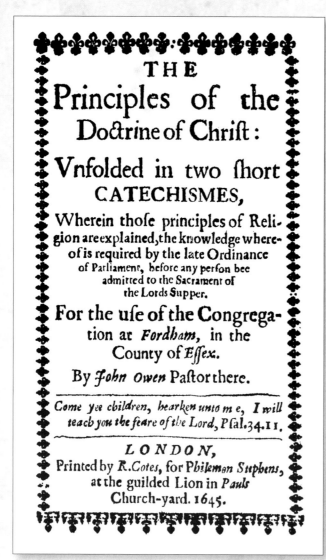

THE
Principles of the
Doctrine of Chrift :
Vnfolded in two ſhort
CATECHISMES,

Wherein thoſe principles of Religion are explained, the knowledge whereof is required by the late Ordinance of Parliament, before any perſon bee admitted to the Sacrament of the Lords Supper.

For the uſe of the Congregation at *Fordham,* in the County of *Eſſex.*

By *John Owen* Paſtor there.

Come yee children, hearken unto me, I will teach you the feare of the Lord, Pſal. 34. 11.

LONDON,
Printed by *R. Cotes,* for *Philemon Stephens,* at the guilded Lion in *Pauls* Church-yard. 1645.

Title page of the original printing of
John Owen's catechisms

In Fordham, Owen realized that the change from the Roman Catholic Church to the Church of England had left many people confused. They needed some help to study the new teachings and be sure of what they believed. To remedy this, Owen wrote two catechisms (a catechism is a book of questions and answers about the basic teachings of a religion), one for young people and one for adults. In them, he explained simply and clearly what the Scriptures teach. He also wrote a small book to help pastors understand and fulfill their duties.

Owen wrote two catechisms and taught them personally to the families he visited regularly.

Owen became well known for his ability to explain Christian teachings with clarity and conviction. When his work in Fordham ended, he was soon invited to become pastor of a congregation of two thousand people in the nearby town of Coggeshall. Owen missed his church family in Fordham but was happy with his new ministry. The church in Coggeshall had benefited from the guidance of some very good pastors, so Owen found himself surrounded by faithful believers who knew the Scriptures and helped and encouraged him in his work.

PHOTO BY ANDREW LUCAS

The church of St. Peter ad Vincula in Coggeshall was one of the largest churches in the area in John Owen's time.

A battle scene of the English Civil War

Owen's fame as a preacher and writer continued to spread so much that he was invited to preach a sermon before Parliament in 1646. This was a great honor. It also happened at a very important time. King Charles had just surrendered to the Scottish army, and the Scots held him captive while the Parliament decided what to do next. In his sermon, Owen talked about the need of bringing the gospel to all men. He also talked about the religious arguments between Christians in England. He explained that wrong teachings cannot be corrected by force. "Cutting off men's heads is no proper remedy for it," he said.

Sir Thomas Fairfax (1612–1671),
commander of Parliament's army

In 1648, after a time of discussion with no true agreement, war broke out again between the king's supporters and Parliament. We call this the Second English Civil War. Soon, a battle that lasted for ten weeks started in a town near Coggeshall, where the Parliament's army surrounded the town until it was victorious. It was a dangerous time for Owen and his church. The leader of the Parliament's army, Lord Fairfax, set up his headquarters in Coggeshall, where he met Owen. The two men became good friends. At the end of the battle, Owen was invited to preach to the troops.

The Second Civil War lasted only three months. Soon, the king's supporters were overpowered, and many were killed. The king was finally taken prisoner, tried, and sentenced to death. On January 30, 1649, he was executed in London. The English people were shocked. They had always seen the king as a representative of God. For many, it seemed that the world was about to end.

The Parliament thought that England should not have a king anymore and that the government should be a republic, in which the people choose their own leaders. Owen thought that the Parliament was right.

The funeral of Charles I

The day after Charles's death, Owen was invited again to preach before Parliament. He wisely did not talk about the awful event. His sermon was so well received that he preached again a few months later. One of his listeners, Oliver Cromwell, was especially impressed with Owen's sermons. Cromwell was a member of Parliament and a very powerful military leader.

A few days later, at a friend's house, Cromwell asked Owen to join him in his next military expedition to Ireland as chaplain for his troops. It was not what Owen wanted to do. He preferred to continue to pastor his church. His congregation in Coggeshall was also not happy to let him go. Cromwell, however, didn't accept refusals and sent a letter to Owen's church practically ordering them to release him from his pastoral duties.

Cromwell asked Owen to join him in his military expedition to Ireland.

CHAPTER THREE

From the Battlefield to the University Halls

Cromwell had a few reasons for wanting to fight in Ireland. Mostly, he was afraid of some rebels who had moved there and were hoping to gain enough supporters to place a new king on the English throne. He also wanted to take revenge because the Irish had killed more than one hundred thousand Protestants. Owen took his responsibility as chaplain seriously, faithfully preaching to the troops, caring for them, and instructing them to study the Scriptures and sing psalms.

Oliver Cromwell (1599–1658)

COURTESY WWW.HERITAGE-HISTORY.COM

Cromwell leading an assault on Drogheda, Ireland

In Ireland, however, Owen was sick most of the time, so he stayed in a castle near Dublin while Cromwell went on to fight. He never saw the terrible attack on the city of Drogheda, where thousands of people, and not just soldiers, were killed.

During his stay in Dublin, Owen visited its famous university, Trinity College. He saw that it needed many repairs and more teachers. As he talked to the people, he found that they were very interested in the gospel but didn't have enough preachers, so he spent many hours in the pulpit.

When he was not teaching and preaching, Owen worked on a book called *The Death of Death in the Death of Christ*. As a pastor, he was always concerned to teach the truth his people needed to know. He realized that what Christ did on the cross was not always clear in people's minds. He wanted them to know that when Christ died, He didn't just make it possible for some people to be saved, but He really secured the salvation of His people.

Finally, Cromwell won the war, but Ireland was left in ruins. About five hundred thousand Irish people were killed by battles and disease, and many were captured as slaves. Back in England, Owen preached again in front of Parliament, asking them to send pastors to Ireland to preach the gospel and start churches. "How is it that Jesus Christ is in Ireland only as a lion staining all His clothes with the blood of His enemies; and there is no one to show that He is a Lamb sprinkled with His own blood for His friends?" he asked.

Owen asked the Parliament to send pastors to Ireland.

Owen followed Cromwell on two more military expeditions—this time to Scotland—both victorious. Soon, he was asked to work as the head of Christ Church College, Oxford, where he had studied many years earlier. At first he didn't feel ready. He had been a country pastor and military chaplain for a long time and was used to speaking to common people. The Parliament insisted, and he finally accepted. The following year, Cromwell became chancellor (or president) of the University of Oxford and promoted Owen to the position of vice-chancellor.

Working at Oxford was not easy. There were many disagreements and problems with money and discipline. Owen worked hard to make things better, even though he was often very sick. This was probably the busiest time in his life. At the same time, he continued to study and write. His personal library was very large, full of all kinds of books—not just about God but also about geography, history, and literature. Whenever he wrote a book, he studied carefully what other Christians had said on the same subject, even those who had different ideas. He knew that God had given him gifts for writing, so he used those gifts for God's glory.

John Owen's personal library

At that time, there were people teaching ideas very different from what the church throughout the centuries had taught, and even the government didn't want these ideas to spread. One group of people in particular, called Socinians, didn't believe that God is one being in three persons, so some of Owen's scholarly books argued against their errors. He also wrote a famous book called *On the Communion with God the Father, the Son, and the Holy Spirit,* which is full of good lessons for Christians. It teaches the importance of the three persons of the Trinity and reminds believers always to keep them in mind during worship and prayer.

The Socinians also taught that God doesn't know everything. For example, they said that He doesn't know who will go to heaven. Owen realized this was a terrible teaching. Not only was it against everything the Bible teaches about God, but it could not bring any comfort. He thought it was horrible to believe that our salvation depends on a decision we, as sinful men, may make rather than on a merciful God. He understood the pain that teaching would bring to parents if their children had died before making a decision. In fact, over half of his children had already died from different causes. Two died around that time from a terrible sickness.

John Owen burying two of his children

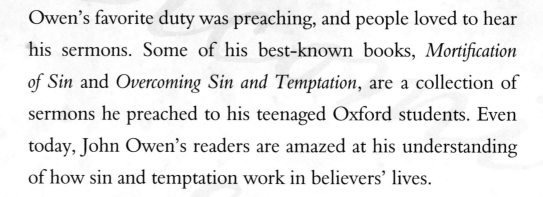

Owen's favorite duty was preaching, and people loved to hear his sermons. Some of his best-known books, *Mortification of Sin* and *Overcoming Sin and Temptation*, are a collection of sermons he preached to his teenaged Oxford students. Even today, John Owen's readers are amazed at his understanding of how sin and temptation work in believers' lives.

As a university professor, Owen refused fancy titles and the traditional cap and hood that Oxford teachers still wear today, because to him they were too similar to the traditions of the Roman Catholic Church. He asked to be called simply John Owen and wore clothes similar to those worn by most young people of his day: a cocked hat, a velvet coat, and Spanish boots with large tops. Some people criticized the way Owen was dressing because they thought it was too fashionable for a minister, but he believed Christians are free to wear what they think is appropriate, as long as it is modest and not worldly.

John Owen's clothes were similar to those worn by most young people of his day.

CHAPTER FOUR
Winds of Persecution

COURTESY WWW.HERITAGE-HISTORY.COM

Cromwell refuses the crown.

In 1653, Oliver Cromwell became Lord Protector of England, Scotland, and Ireland (which meant that he was the head of those countries). Three years later, a majority of Parliament suggested that he should be crowned as king. Cromwell thought about it for a while. Owen was shocked. Cromwell had always wanted a republic!

How could he even think of becoming king? Some people wrote a paper against this idea, and Owen readily signed it. Later, Cromwell refused the crown. At the same time, he was not happy to hear that Owen had been so opposed to the idea.

A few months later, when Cromwell resigned as chancellor of Oxford, passing on the position to his son Richard, Owen lost his job of vice-chancellor. Eventually, he stopped preaching at St. Mary's Church and returned to his birthplace, Stadhampton, where he was welcomed as a pastor.

COURTESY OF THE CROMWELL MUSEUM, HUNTINGTON, ENGLAND

Richard Cromwell (1628–1712)

Oliver Cromwell died in 1658, but Owen was not called to his side. Soon, Cromwell's son Richard took his father's place as Lord Protector of England, but it was obvious that he was not able to run a country. Finally, he quit. Without a king and a Lord Protector, the whole country was in turmoil.

In 1660, Charles II, son of Charles I, was invited to return to the throne. People rejoiced. There were music and laughter, and the streets were decorated and strewn with flowers. The Puritans were afraid that Charles II would be just like his father, but he reassured them and promised religious freedom. Within two years, however, he became even stricter than his father, demanding again that everyone conform to the Book of Common Prayer. This was known as the Act of Uniformity. Under the Act of Uniformity people were not free to worship according to the teachings found in the Bible, but only according to the rules established by the government.

King Charles II (1630–1685)

PHOTO BY MARTIN BEEK

King Charles II gave all pastors and preachers until August 24, 1662, to make a decision. Those who refused to obey his religious rules would be fined and forbidden to preach forever. On that day, almost two thousand pastors preached their last sermon to their congregations as they prepared to leave them, facing a future of poverty and persecution. Many left the country and moved to other European countries or to America. That day is known as the Great Ejection.

COURTESY OF WWW.REFORMATIONART.COM

Puritans fleeing England

Some of Owen's friends visited him at Stadhampton to discuss the situation. They concluded that the way the king wanted them to worship was contrary to the Scriptures and that they had to obey God—even if it meant disobeying the king. John immediately wrote a booklet entitled *Discourse Concerning Liturgies*, where he explained that the government should not demand that churches repeat some words stated in a human book. Knowing that disobeying the king was going to be very dangerous, he sent his wife and children to a safer place as guests of Charles Fleetwood, one of Cromwell's old generals.

At first many Puritans kept worshiping as they believed was right by meeting privately in homes, but the king added a law saying that no more than five people could hold a religious meeting in a home, unless they were all part of the same family. This law was called the Conventicle Act.

Most Puritan pastors stopped preaching but continued to visit individual families, until the king added a new law saying that Puritan preachers and pastors could not come within five miles of a congregation where they had preached before. This law was called the Five Mile Act. Five miles was a long way in those days because there were no cars. All those pastors were then out of a job and forced to stay away from the congregations they loved. Many suffered hunger and became so poor that they lost their homes.

Lord Clarendon (1609–1674)

The man in charge of enforcing these harsh laws was Lord Edward Hyde of Clarendon. Lord Clarendon admired Owen and visited him twice to persuade him to write an answer to some strong accusations made by the Roman Catholic Church. Lord Clarendon also promised Owen great favors if he would conform to the king's way of worship. Owen agreed to write, but could not conform.

41

Because he would not conform to the king's way of worship, Owen often ran into serious dangers. Once, when he was visiting some friends near Oxford, he barely escaped some guards who had come to capture him because the lady of the house, thinking he had already left, sent them away. Another time, as he was preaching in his house to a congregation of about thirty people, the king's guards came in, threw everyone out, and searched every room. Owen was a very important man in England, so they didn't put him in jail.

The king's guards caught John Owen as he was preaching in his house.

CHAPTER FIVE
England's Dark Hour

In 1665, the plague, a terrible illness carried by fleas, spread all over London. The Parliament and the court moved to other palaces, and the nobles and rich people to their country homes. Even most of the doctors and preachers left the city. Soon everyone else tried to leave London, but the king ordered that the gates be closed to anyone who didn't have a certificate of health, so that the disease would not spread to other cities. During the summer, as many as six thousand people died every week. It was the worst plague London had ever experienced. It is still known today as the Great Plague of London.

The next year, just when the plague had almost died down, a fire started in one area of London and spread through the city at an amazing speed, destroying almost every building. People ran to the river trying to save their lives. The fire lasted four days and nights, destroying about four-fifths of the city. This is known as the Great Fire of London.

To top it all, around that time England lost an important war at sea against Holland. It was a terrible time, and people were very discouraged.

The Great Fire of London

Owen, like most Puritan preachers, went to London after the fire to preach to a small group of believers. A few years later, when another preacher died, his congregation joined with John Owen's, united in one church. Preachers in London had some freedom because the authorities didn't really want to go to London at that time. Also, they were afraid because many people believed that the plague, the fire, and the lost battle were punishments from God for the way England had treated the Puritans. Still, Owen was often in danger, especially during his travels.

When he was not preaching, Owen spent most of his time studying and writing to help people understand the Word of God. He also wrote letters to influential men to convince them to allow religious freedom. He was very well known and admired in England, and when he wrote, people paid attention. Even the king invited him a few times to discuss different issues, and each time Owen begged him to allow Puritan preachers to continue their ministry.

King Charles II invited John Owen to discuss different issues.

At a time when Christians in England were very divided among themselves, Owen encouraged peace and unity. To a government official he wrote, "It seems that we are some of the first who ever, anywhere in the world, from the foundation of it, thought of ruining and destroying persons of the same religion with ourselves," only because they choose to worship in a different way.

In 1672, the king finally released a declaration that gave the Puritans some freedom to worship and preach. Sadly, this freedom didn't last long, because the Parliament, afraid that the king was becoming Roman Catholic, persuaded him once again to enforce the old restrictive laws.

It seems that we are some of the first who ever, anywhere in the world, from the foundation of it, thought of ruining and destroying persons of the

John Bunyan (1628–1688)

It was during that short period of freedom that a good friend of Owen's, the preacher John Bunyan, author of *The Pilgrim's Progress*, was released from prison. John Owen had tried for years to convince the king to free Bunyan and now helped him publish his book, which is one of the most well-known Christian books in the world. One story says that the king asked John Owen why a great man like him, who was famous all over England for his knowledge and intelligence, was so interested in John Bunyan, a simple man with little schooling, who had made his living fixing pots from town to town. To this John Owen replied that if he could have Bunyan's abilities for preaching to the common people, he would gladly give up all his learning.

49

CHAPTER SIX

John Owen's Last Years

In 1675, Owen's wife, Mary, died. It must have been a terrible day for Owen, who had already lost all of his eleven children. After eighteen months, he married a widow, Dorothy D'Oyley. She came from a rich family, and Owen now had enough money to live comfortably. Some people criticized him because he traveled with a horse and buggy, which was like having a fancy car today. Owen didn't think it was wrong to have nice things or money if they were used responsibly, keeping in mind the needs of other people.

One day, as Owen was traveling, two people stopped him and captured his horses. They were informers, people who had made a living of catching Puritan preachers and reporting them to the authorities. These informers were particularly violent, and soon a crowd gathered on the scene to see what was happening. Right then, a judge passed by and, seeing that the informers had not behaved correctly, he settled the matter at the house of another judge, and Owen was set free.

Two informers stopped John Owen as he traveled.

At the same time, Owen had many problems with his health, especially asthma, which made it difficult for him to breathe. Finally, he retired in the quiet village of Ealing (now part of London), where he spent his last days. The day before his death, he wrote his dear friend Charles Fleetwood, "I am going to Him whom my soul loveth, or rather who has loved me with an everlasting love. I am leaving the ship of the church in a storm; but while the great Pilot [Jesus] is in it, the loss of a poor under-rower [John Owen] will be inconsiderable [unimportant]."

On the morning of John Owen's death, a friend, William Payne, came to give him the good news that his last book, *Meditations on the Glory of Christ*, was ready to be published. "I am glad to hear it," replied Owen; "but, O brother Payne, the long wished for day is come at last, in which I shall see that glory in another manner than I have ever done, or was capable of doing, in this world." John Owen died that afternoon. It was August 24, 1683, exactly twenty-one years after the Great Ejection.

John Owen explains that he will soon see Christ's glory.

During his life, John Owen was much respected. People knew that he was truthful and fair in considering other opinions. They knew that he studied hard and thought thoroughly about everything he said. They especially relied on him as a defender of the truth as it is written in the Bible, against all those who wanted to change it.

At the same time, Owen knew that even the great mind God had given him could never understand fully everything that God has communicated to men. That's why his writings are always very humble and sincere. When you read them, you feel that you are talking with a close friend who cares for your soul and for God's glory. This is why they have inspired many men and women throughout the centuries. Charles Spurgeon, one of the greatest preachers of all times, called John Owen "the Prince of Puritans." The inscription on his grave calls him "a traveller on earth who grasped God like one in heaven."

John Owen's books and sermons are not always easy for us to read today because they were written in an old-fashioned form of the English language, but there are some simpler versions in print, and you can ask your parents to read some passages to you.

Time Line of John Owen's Life

1616— John Owen is born.

1628— He enters college.

1633— William Laud becomes Archbishop of Canterbury.

1635— John Owen receives his master's degree.

1637— He leaves Oxford University.

1642— The English Civil War begins. Owen moves to London, where a sermon changes his life. He writes his first book.

1643— Owen receives the call to be a pastor in Fordham, where he marries Mary Rooke.

1646— Owen preaches before Parliament; the Westminster Confession is written.

1649— King Charles I is executed. Oliver Cromwell takes John Owen to Ireland as his chaplain.

1651— Owen starts working at Oxford University.

1657— He opposes an attempt to make Cromwell king.

1658— Oliver Cromwell dies.

1660— Owen leaves Oxford.

1662— Nonconformist pastors are forbidden to preach.

1665— The Great Plague spreads through London.

1666— The Great London Fire destroys thousands of homes.

1672— Temporary Declaration of Indulgence by the king gives some religious freedom.

1675— Owen's first wife, Mary, dies.

1676— He marries Dorothy D'Oyley.

1683— John Owen dies.

Did you know?

❧ Oliver Cromwell created a New Model Army, which seemed unbeatable. One of the reasons for its success was that Cromwell chose his officers according to their abilities and not their title. Before that, officers usually came from rich or noble families. Cromwell wanted courageous men who knew how to fight and lead others, even if they were poor. He also wanted men who were strong believers.

Another difference was the type of armor worn by the soldiers, especially horsemen. Before, horsemen wore a full armor, which would slow down the horses. In the New Model Army, they wore only thick leather jackets. Soon they were nicknamed Ironsides, because they could ride through an enemy army like the blade of a sword.

A third reason for the success of Cromwell's army is that he taught his men that they should never chase after a fleeing enemy. Instead, they should regroup and ride back into the battle. This is something the king's army didn't usually do. This way, after an initial victory, Cromwell kept his men formed and could use them again.

❧ During the war, the two parties gave each other nicknames. The supporters of the Parliament called the supporters of the king Cavaliers, an ancient name for horsemen. This might have been because, until the New Model Army was formed, the Cavaliers were considered to have by far the best cavalry. On the other hand, the supporters of the king called the others Roundheads, maybe because many of them wore their hair shorter than the Cavaliers.

❧ Cromwell and Owen were concerned about the suffering of Christians in other nations. When the Duke of Savoy fought and killed over 1,500 Protestant men, women, and children in the Italian Alps, Cromwell used his influence to ask him to stop the persecution, and both Cromwell and Owen helped collect money to help the survivors.

❧ The Scottish people had been on the side of the Parliament against Charles I because they believed that the king should allow all Christians to worship as they thought was right, but they were shocked by Charles's execution. They didn't think a king should be put to death and believed that England should still have a king. So the Scottish leaders talked to Charles II,

son of Charles I. They were willing to help him become king of Scotland and England if he promised to allow religious freedom. Charles promised, and the Scottish leaders prepared to fight Cromwell. They were surprised to find that Cromwell's army was too strong to defeat.

His army being scattered, Charles II became a fugitive. Many wanted to capture him because Cromwell had offered a thousand pounds to anyone who would give the king into his hands. Charles cut off his long hair, dressed as a farmer, and found refuge at the house of some poor woodcutters who were loyal to him. Once, his hosts thought that some soldiers were coming to search their house and warned Charles, who fled into some thick woods and climbed up into an oak tree. There he stayed all day, until his hosts found him another place to stay. Eventually, he fled to France, where his mother and siblings had already found refuge.

He returned to London on May 29, 1660, which was also his birthday, to be crowned King Charles II. In some places in England, boys and girls wear sprigs of oak on that day in his memory.

❧ Most of the time, Owen and his family probably traveled by coach. Coaches were usually drawn by two, four, or six horses. By 1600, there were so many coaches in London that people were complaining about traffic jams. A bill was introduced to limit the use of coaches, but it did not pass. When people traveled from one city to another by coach, they usually covered thirty to forty miles per day.

❧ Someone who lived at the same time as Owen described him as tall and hand-some. He looked and behaved like a gentleman. At the same time, he was very kind and friendly. People liked to talk to him. He liked to joke with his friends, without going too far. He was normally quite calm. He didn't get excited when he received honor, praise, or material things and was not depressed by troubles and difficulties.

❧ Charles I and his wife, Henrietta, loved high fashion. Charles wore his hair lon-ger on the left side, as that was stylish in those days. Charles II, who spent much of his life in exile in France, returned to England wearing a full wig of dark, long, and curly hair. The fashion of using pow-der to lighten and perfume the hair, as John Owen used to do, didn't become widespread until the eighteenth century, when white hair became the rage for both young and old.

❧ The University of Oxford is the old-est university in the English-speaking world. During the Civil War, the univer-sity was a center for the Royalist Party (the supporters of the king), but the city of Oxford was on the side of the Parliament. For the period of the war, though, the city of Oxford was secured as the king's headquarters.

✤ Most of the 102 passengers who left Plymouth, England, on September 16, 1620, on the famous ship *Mayflower* were Puritans looking for religious freedom. They had made some attempts to leave earlier on two separate ships, the *Mayflower* and the *Speedwell*. The *Speedwell*, however, could not make it due to leaks. During the difficult trip, two passengers died, and two were born. They landed in America late in 1620, in the area that is now called Massachusetts. We call the place where they landed Plymouth Rock. Much later, some of the Puritan churches in America asked John Owen to join them, but he refused, probably feeling that he was more needed in England.

✤ London was a busy city in Owen's day, but it looked very different from how it looks today. Most of the houses were made out of wood and were built very close to each other. The streets were narrow and crowded. It was not a clean place, and much dirty water ran through the streets into the river Thames. In those crowded and dirty surroundings, it was easy for the plague to spread.

The wooden houses were also a terrible fire hazard. Just a spark at the house of the king's baker on Pudding Lane near London Bridge resulted in the terrible destruction of most of the city. The smell of smoke at 2:00 a.m. woke up the baker's assistant, who called all the family, but it was too late.

A Modern Version of John Owen's
Lesser Catechism

EDITED BY MICHAEL BROWN

1. *Q. From where do we learn all truth about God and ourselves?*
A. From the Holy Bible, the Word of God.

2. *Q. What does the Bible teach us about God?*
A. That He is an eternal, infinite, most holy Spirit, who has created all things and does with them whatsoever He pleases.

3. *Q. Is there only one God?*
A. One only in His essence and being, but one in three distinct persons: Father, Son, and Holy Spirit.

4. *Q. What else does the Bible teach us about God that we ought to know?*
A. His decrees and His works.

5. *Q. What are God's decrees concerning us?*

A. His eternal purposes of saving some by Jesus Christ, for the praise of His glory, and of condemning others for their sins.

6. *Q. What are the works of God?*
A. Acts or doings of His power, whereby He creates, sustains, and governs all things.

7. *Q. What does almighty God require of us?*
A. Holy and spiritual obedience, according to the law He gave us.

8. *Q. Are we able to do this ourselves?*
A. No, in no way, for we are sinful by nature and cannot do good works.

9. *Q. Since God first created humans righteous, innocent, and in His own image, how did we become sinful?*

A. By the fall of our first parents, who broke God's covenant and brought upon us His curse.

10. Q. *How can we be delivered from this terrible situation?*
A. Only by Jesus Christ.

11. Q. *Who is Jesus Christ?*
A. God and man united in one person, to be a mediator between God and man.

12. Q. *What is He to us?*
A. A king, a priest, and a prophet.

13. Q. *How is He a king to us?*
A. By converting us to God by His Spirit, subduing us to His obedience, and ruling over us by His grace.

14. Q. *How is He a priest to us?*
A. By offering up Himself an acceptable sacrifice on the cross, so satisfying the justice of God for our sins, removing His curse from us, and bringing us to Him.

15. Q. *How is He a prophet to us?*
A. By revealing to our hearts, from the bosom of His Father, the way and truth whereby we must come to Him.

16. Q. *In what condition does Jesus Christ perform these offices of king, priest, and prophet?*
A. First in a low state of humiliation on earth, but now in a glorious state of exaltation in heaven.

17. Q. *For whom does Christ perform all these?*
A. Only for His elect.

18. Q. *What is the church of Christ?*
A. The universal company of God's elect, called to be His adopted children.

19. Q. *How do we become members of this church?*
A. By a living faith.

20. Q. *What is a living faith?*
A. An assured resting of the soul upon God's promises of mercy in Jesus Christ, for pardon of sins now and glory later.

21. Q. *How do we get this faith?*
A. By the effectual working of the Spirit of God in our hearts, freely calling us from the state of nature to the state of grace.

22. Q. *Does God consider us righteous because of our faith?*
A. No, but only for the righteousness of

Christ, freely imputed to us, and received by faith.

23. Q. *Is there anything required of us besides faith?*
A. Yes, repentance also and holiness.

24. Q. *What is repentance?*
A. A forsaking of all sin, with godly sorrow for what we have committed.

25. Q. *What is the holiness which God requires of us?*
A. Universal obedience to the will of God revealed to us.

26. Q. *What are the privileges of believers?*
A. First, union with Christ; second, adoption as God's children; third, communion of saints; fourth, right to the seals of the new covenant; fifth, Christian liberty; sixth, resurrection of the body to life eternal.

27. Q. *What are the sacraments, or seals, of the new covenant?*
A. Visible seals of God's spiritual promises, made to us in the blood of Jesus Christ.

28. *Which ones are they?*
A. Baptism and the Lord's Supper.

29. Q. *What is baptism?*
A. A holy ordinance, whereby, being sprinkled with water according to Christ's institution, we are by His grace made children of God and have the promises of the covenant sealed to us.

30. Q. *What is the Lord's Supper?*
A. A holy ordinance of Christ, appointed to communicate to believers His body and blood spiritually, being represented by bread and wine, blessed, broken, poured out, and received by them.

31. Q. *Who has a right to this sacrament?*
A. Only those who trust in Jesus Christ by faith.

32. Q. *What is the communion of saints?*
A. A holy union between all God's people, partakers of the same Spirit, and members of the same mystical body.

33. *What is the end of all this?*
A. The glory of God in our salvation.

Glory be to God on high!

Acknowledgments

I am first of all grateful to God for allowing me to finish another book. Each time, I receive so much help and encouragement from others that I feel that my part is actually very small. As usual, I thank my husband, Tom, and my children, Christian, Simon, Dustin, David, Jonathan, Kevin, Raphael, and Renaissance for their support and for putting up with my endless questions.

I also thank my church family at Christ URC, Santee, California, for their continual encouragement. I especially thank my pastor, Rev. Michael G. Brown, who has done extensive academic research on John Owen, for his precious advice, his careful review, and for introducing me to his brother Matt, who has masterfully illustrated this book. Rev. Brown has also produced a modern version of John Owen's Lesser Catechism, which appears at the end of this book.

I thank Dr. Carl R. Trueman, Professor of Historical Theology and Church History, Westminster Seminary, Philadelphia; Dr. Kelly M. Kapic, Professor of Theological Studies, Covenant College; Rev. Michael Matossian, Pastor of Emmanuel Orthodox Presbyterian Church, Wilmington, Delaware, for reviewing this book; and Mark Turnbull, author of the historical novel *Decision Most Deadly*, for kindly reviewing and contributing to the last section, "Did You Know?".

I am deeply touched by the generosity of all those who have allowed me to use their photos.

I am also grateful to all those who have written words of encouragement about this series and for the relentless support of the staff at Reformation Heritage Books, particularly Jay Collier and Steve Renkema, who never cease to amaze me for their patience, wisdom, and commitment to quality.